FRESHWATER FISHING

FISHING TECHNIQUES, BAIT AND TACKLE EXPLAINED, AND GAME FISH TIPS

T0166274

Dave Bosanko

Adventure Skills Guides

CATCH FISH LIKE A PRO

Adventure Skills Guides

Fishing is a great activity for anyone who can get near the water, and this Adventure Skills Guide will get you fishing without all the fuss. It introduces you to everything from the differences between rods and reels and the ways you can rig up a rod to where to find fish, tips on how to hook them, and even a recipe for cooking your catch. Once you start fishing, it can become an enjoyable challenge that lasts a lifetime or a simple pastime that helps you get out into nature. So grab your tacklebox and get out on the water!

HOW TO USE THIS GUIDE

This guide is intuitively organized so you can quickly find the information you want. It begins with everything you need to get started, from a checklist about safety and fishing regulations to the basics of rods, reels, and tackle. This guide also includes directions on how to set up a number of common fishing rigs as well as tips on how to entice, hook, and land your fish. If you're searching for tips on how to catch a specific species, turn to the "Fishing Tips" section for advice on how to locate and catch bass, panfish, walleye, and more. Finally, if you've caught a fish and want to take it home, turn toward the end of the guide for tips on filleting and cooking your catch.

DAVE BOSANKO

Dave Bosanko is an avid fisherman and naturalist with degrees in Biology and Chemistry from the University of Kansas. He spent a long career at the University of Minnesota's field stations before retiring. In addition to fishing, he enjoys hiking, sailing, and building small wooden boats. Much of his time is now spent writing or visiting natural areas in the U.S. and beyond.

Cover and book design by Lora Westberg
Edited by Brett Ortler

Cover image: Northern Pike by Rocksweeper/Shutterstock.

All images copyrighted.
All illustrations by Jonathan Norberg except cinch knots by Steve Jones, and J Hook, Circle Hook and Treble Hook on pg. 9 by Dmitry Rubanik/Shutterstock.
Photo credits on gatefold

10 9 8 7 6 5 4 3 2

Freshwater Fishing: Fishing Techniques, Bait and Tackle Explained, and Game Fish Tips
Copyright © 2020 by Dave Bosanko
Published by Adventure Publications, an imprint of AdventureKEEN
(800) 678-7006
www.adventurepublications.net
All rights reserved
Printed in China
ISBN: 978-1-59193-959-7

BE SAFE

Landing a big fish is no reward if you come home with a bad sunburn or a bandaged hand. With care, even small children can have fun and stay safe when fishing, but like anything else, fishing can be potentially hazardous. Before you head out, run through this checklist.

☐ Before you leave for the lake (and on your way back after fishing's done), check your rods for dangling hooks. They are an easy way to inadvertently land a catch you don't want: kids or the family dog.

☐ Life jackets are a must for everyone in a boat, and they are a great idea for young children on the shore or on a dock. Always make sure that they are properly fitted. To check, lift the child by the shoulders of their life jacket with their arms raised above their head. If they slip out of it or their chin/ears slip through, it's not the right fit.

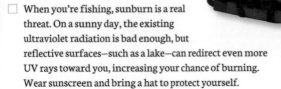

☐ When you're fishing, sunburn is a real threat. On a sunny day, the existing ultraviolet radiation is bad enough, but reflective surfaces—such as a lake—can redirect even more UV rays toward you, increasing your chance of burning. Wear sunscreen and bring a hat to protect yourself.

☐ Bug spray is a must, especially in the height of mosquito season. Biting flies can be a real pain, as well, so dress accordingly.

BE LEGAL

☐ In most states, adults need to be carrying a fishing license when angling, but kids may not. Check your state's regulations for details.

☐ Game fish populations are carefully regulated, and there are limits on the size or number of fish that anglers can legally take or possess. There are also limits on when you can fish. Seasons and limits vary by state (and even by body of water), so when you get your license, get a copy of your state's fishing regulations, read it, and then keep it with your tackle. Regulations are revised annually, so be sure to stay up to date. To help you measure your catch, keep a small tape measure with your tackle.

Black Crappie

BEFORE YOU LEAVE, CHECK YOUR GEAR

☐ **Rods and Reels:** Inspect your rods and reels before you leave; you don't want to end up on the lake with a broken rod from your last time out.

☐ **Tackle:** Do you need to replace any gear or equipment? Did you remember to pack that new pink-and-green never-fail lure you bought the other day and put on the kitchen table?

☐ **Knife:** Whether you're cutting off a lure or cutting bait, chances are you'll need a knife for something while you're fishing.

☐ **Bait:** Do you need fresh bait? What did you do with the live bait left over from the last trip? Worms, leeches, and crickets can be kept alive in the refrigerator for a time, but extended stays (or worse, exposure to the sun/elements) can make them spoil in a hurry.

☐ **Pliers and Clippers:** Needle-nose pliers are a necessity for removing deeply embedded hooks. Fingernail clippers are also very handy to have when snipping monofilament line.

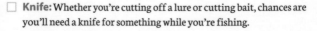

TACKLE

Tackle can refer to any piece of equipment used to catch fish, but in general, the word refers to terminal tackle: equipment that attaches to the end of a line on a rod, such as weights, hooks, and lures. Tackle is usually carried in tackle boxes, but anglers on shore often use a bucket.

FISHING RODS

Fishing rods help you do several things: cast a line, set the hook, and fight the fish. They also have a fourth, more subtle, purpose: they help you feel what is happening on the end of your line when it's in the water.

Rods are matched to the kind of reel you are using, as well as the fishing conditions and the size of fish you are targeting. Most rods contain some writing near the handle; these provide recommendations for line size and lure weight. When pairing rods and reels, be sure the combination feels balanced and comfortable in your hand. If you're just starting out, buy a combination reel-and-rod set. Such rigs often even come with line already spooled, making it about as hassle-free as it gets.

> **Baitcasting Rods:** Baitcasting rods are typically 4 to 8 feet long. They either have a short handle at the base of the rod or a two-part handle. Many baitcasting rods have a trigger-like protrusion where your index finger rests while holding the rod. The eyes on baitcasting rods are all close to the same size.
>
> You can mount either a spincasting reel or a baitcasting reel on a baitcasting rod.

Spinning Rods: Spinning rods are 4 to 12 feet long and have long handles with the reel mounted partway up the handle. Spinning reels hang under the rod and you hold the stock of the reel between your first and second finger. To reduce drag on the line when casting, the eyes on spinning rods are larger near the reel and get smaller toward the tip.

Fly Fishing Rods: Fly rods are 5 to 12 feet long, with long handles and eyes of about equal size. Fly reels are mounted under and at the base of the rod. You hold the rod with your hand a few inches above the reel. The size of a fly rod depends on the weight of the line to be cast.

REELS

All reels have two basic functions: to hold your fishing line and to help you land a fish. The line is either wound directly onto a spool that turns, or is wound around a fixed spool using a moving mechanism. Rods also have knobs or controls to adjust drag; this helps keep tension on the line, but when a fish hits hard, it also enables the line to slip somewhat, preventing the line from breaking.

Spincast Reels (Closed-face, push-button): Spincast reels are the simplest reels to use and most trouble- free. Spincast reels have a fixed spool and a mechanism that wraps the line around the spool when the crank is turned. The spool, and the wrapping mechanism, are all enclosed. The thumb button on the back of the reel is used to control line release when casting. These reels are simple to use, durable, inexpensive, and a good choice for beginners and children.

Spinning Reels (Open-faced): Spinning reels have a fixed spool with the line wrapped around it. The line is put on the spool and held there by a mechanism called the bail. Spinning reels are used on spinning rods and are mounted below the rod. To cast, you open the bail, hold the line with your finger during the cast, and release it at the end of the cast. With a little practice, spinning reels are easy to use; they are the most versatile and common reel variety.

Baitcasting Reels: On baitcasting reels, the spool rotates, taking up line as the crank turns; these reels are mounted on top of baitcasting rods. These reels are the most complicated to use as it's easy to create a "bird's nest" in which the line becomes entangled when casting. Baitcasting reels are preferred for landing large, strong fish, or for very precise casts when fishing amid trees, vegetation, and other cover.

Fly Fishing Reels: These reels are mainly for holding line, not fighting fish. The line goes directly onto a rotating spool with a simple crank system. Fly fishing reels have no, or very simple drag system for fighting fish.

Fishing Line: Fishing line is matched to rods and reels, fishing conditions, and fishing style. Fishing lines are described by their breaking point (test) and the material they are made of. Six-pound-test line breaks with six pounds of pull. There are three basic kinds of line with many variations on each (monofilament, braided and fly line). Monofilament is by far the most common and versatile. A fishing rod's ability to flex, and its reel's drag, allows anglers to land fish heavier than the pound test of their line. In general, a 6–12 pound test is a good fit for most fishing setups. When selecting line, keep in mind that good-quality line holds knots better, kinks less, and lasts longer than cheap line. Over time, line wears down and becomes weaker. Removing a couple yards from the end of your line after several fishing trips is a good idea.

SPOOLING A REEL

Putting line on a reel can be a little fussy, but if you don't do it right, the line won't come off the reel correctly and will often become kinked or twisted. Many sporting goods stores and bait shops sell line from bulk spools and they will spool the line for you for free, which is a good way to go, as line needs to be wound on the spool the right way and the spool not overfilled.

How to Spool Line for Spincast and Spinning Reels

With a little care, it is not too hard to spool line at home too.

- Start by tying the end of the line around the reel's spool; if you're using a spinning reel, make sure the bail is open.

- Set the spool of line on the floor so it does not spin; the line will come off the spool counterclockwise.

- Crank the reel with one hand and, with the fingers of your other hand, trap the line snugly against the rod as you crank; the line should go onto the spool clockwise.

- Make sure the line is tightly spooled on the reel, but don't overfill it.

- Once you're done, you can thread the line up through the eyelets of the rod.

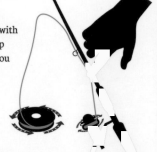

How to Spool Line for Baitcasting and Fly Fishing R.eels

- Pass the line through the pages of a thick book.

- Have a helper hold the spool of new line on a screwdriver, with the line coming off the bottom of the spool.

- Crank the line onto the reel, and make sure it is tight.

- Once you're done, you can thread the line up through the eyelets of the rod.

HOOKS

The most important part of a fishing hook is its point; it must be very sharp and protrude out from the bait. Dull or bent hooks catch few fish. But you don't need to worry about fish seeing the hook; they often eat sharp, spiny things (other fish!), so hooks fit into their environment.

There are two basic styles of hooks: J hooks and circle hooks.

J Hooks: These are the hooks you're probably familiar with, the straight part of the J (known as the shank) can vary in length and shape, depending on the bait one plans to use. To set a hook when a fish bites a J hook, you jerk the line hard.

J Hook

Circle Hooks: These are new to recreational fishing, but commercial fishermen have used them for years. They are curled without a straight shank and at first glance it looks like they wouldn't work. But they do, and they are probably the best all-around hook. In particular, circle hooks have great holding power; once embedded in a fish they rarely come out. Circle hooks most commonly lodge in the corner of the fish's mouth, which helps improve fish survival once it's released. To set the hook when using a circle hook, you steadily tighten and pull on the line (it will not set properly if it's jerked).

Circle Hook

Treble Hooks: Treble hooks are essentially three J hooks in one; treble hooks have multiple points and are often attached to lures.

Treble Hook

An assortment of lures

SINKERS

Sinkers are weights used to get the bait underwater quickly, and to hold it in place if there is a current. Sinkers range from split shot that is just a fraction of an ounce to bottom-bouncers that are many ounces. It's generally best to use the least amount of weight possible. Many sinkers are made of lead, but because lost sinkers are consumed by fish, birds, and other wildlife, non-lead sinkers are increasing in popularity.

Sinkers are either fixed in one place on the line (often pinched onto the line), or they slide on the line. Sliding sinkers allow a fish to run with the bait but not feel the drag of the sinker.

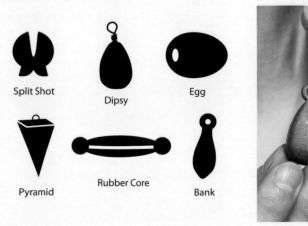

Split Shot

Dipsy

Egg

Pyramid

Rubber Core

Bank

SWIVELS

Swivels come in three common forms: barrels, clips, and three-ways. Barrel swivels have two loops that spin independently, allowing terminal tackle to spin without twisting the line. Clip swivels also spin but have a clip at one end for quick attachment to other tackle. Three-way swivels have three independently spinning loops that help keep dropped lines from twisting. Like line, swivels are sized by pounds of test. Always use a swivel that's a size heavier than the test of your line; this will ensure that they don't fail before the line does.

Three-way

Barrel

Clip

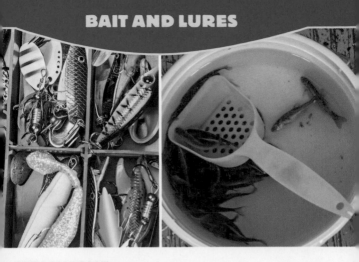

TYPES OF LIVE BAIT

The surest way for a beginner to catch fish is to use live bait. When it comes to live bait, presentation (how it looks in the water) is key. The overall best choice for live bait is a plump worm, with an active minnow coming in as a close second. Crawfish, leeches, frogs, grasshoppers, and crickets are also great options. The new plastic imitation baits that are soaked in attractant sometimes out-fish the real thing, but not often. Many states now have regulations regarding the disposal of unused live bait; don't dump your minnow pail into the lake. Instead, dispose of it on land in the garbage.

There are two different ways to present live bait to fish: suspended between the surface and the bottom, or by fishing on the bottom. There is an overwhelming amount of "terminal tackle" (tackle that goes onto the end of your line) designed to accomplish this and an even more overwhelming number of ways to attach that tackle, but they are all variations on a basic pattern.

HOW TO HOOK LIVE BAIT

When using live bait, you want it to appear as natural as possible, and keep the bait alive for as long as you can. Here are some popular ways to hook bait.

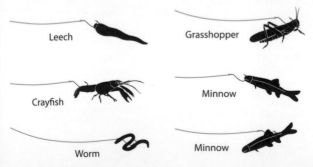

Leech

Grasshopper

Crayfish

Minnow

Worm

Minnow

Suspended Rigs: In a suspended rig, the bait is held in the water column by a bobber. Bobbers, also known as floats, are used to hold the bait at a specific depth. Floats come in many different shapes, sizes, and colors, with different kinds of mechanisms to attach them to the line. Bobbers need to be just big enough to hold up the sinker and bait, but have the least resistance possible when the fish pulls it under. Long slender bobbers have less resistance when pulled under the water when compared to round ones. The color of floats (they are often bright orange or red) is mostly a matter of visibility for the angler and has little effect on the fish. Most bobbers are fixed in one position on the line (and depth is adjusted by moving it), but some (known as slip bobbers) slide on the line and the depth is set with a bobber stop.

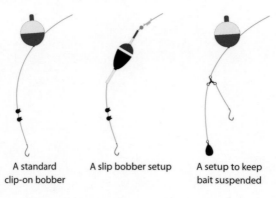

A standard
clip-on bobber

A slip bobber setup

A setup to keep
bait suspended

Bottom Rigs: When targeting some species, you'll want to keep your bait close to the bottom. Both fixed and sliding weights can be used to keep bait on the bottom. A sliding sinker allows the fish to run with the bait and not feel its resistance. Use the smallest weight that will keep your bait where you want it on the bottom. Three-way rigs are best when fishing in streams or rivers to hold the bait up in the current.

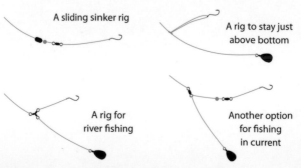

A sliding sinker rig

A rig to stay just
above bottom

A rig for
river fishing

Another option
for fishing
in current

HOW TO RIG A FLOAT/BOBBER

A float/bobber rod is often the first introduction to fishing. Simple to set up and versatile enough to target a number of fish species, it's a good option for beginners, kids, and the experienced alike.

What You Need

To set up a float rod, you'll need a bobber stop (these are sold pre-tied around small plastic sleeves), a plastic bead, a small sinker, and a hook.

Step 1

Start by loosening the line to give you some slack to work with. Take the line from the end of the rod, and pull the end of the line through the sleeve of the bobber stop.

Step 2

Pull the bobber stop thread onto the line, and pull both ends tight. (Discard the plastic sleeve.)

Placing and tying the bobber stop

Step 3

Put a bead below the bobber stop (it ensures the bobber stop doesn't pass through), then thread the line through the bobber.

Step 4

Tie on your hook (see the back of this book for knot-tying instructions), clip off the excess line with a fingernail clipper, and affix a small split shot or two below the bobber. That's it: you're ready to fish! To adjust the depth of your bobber, you simply slide the bobber stop up and down the line.

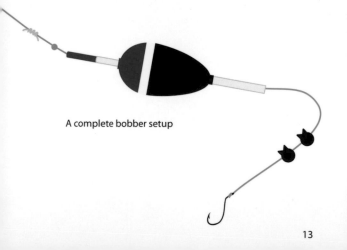

A complete bobber setup

LURES

Lures are designed to mimic aquatic prey, often injured, as they pass through the water. They don't have to look like a baitfish to work. A soup spoon with a hook attached may not look like a minnow, and a spinner bait may not resemble a fish, but when pulled through the water, the disturbance they make appears to be a fleeing baitfish.

Lures are all about movement and presentation, not just flinging them at the water. It takes some practice to choose the right lure for the conditions at hand and then to make it dance just right.

Lures are attached directly to the end of your line, often with a leader or a swivel clip. If you want your lure to appear as natural as possible (say, if you're using a lure that resembles a fish or other prey item), tying the lure directly is best. But if you're using a big flashy plug or a spinning lure, swivel clips are a good option. Under some conditions, if you want to keep a lure near the bottom, you'll need to add a sinker.

SOME LURE SETUPS

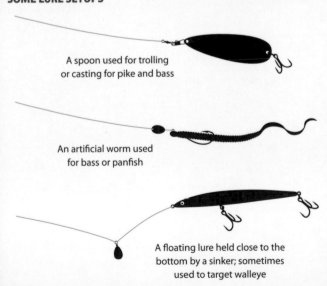

A spoon used for trolling or casting for pike and bass

An artificial worm used for bass or panfish

A floating lure held close to the bottom by a sinker; sometimes used to target walleye

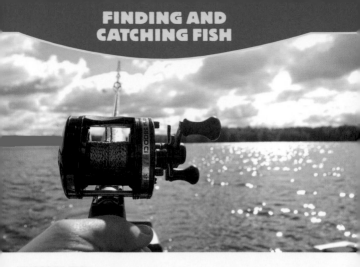

WHERE TO FISH

Start out by paying attention to where others are fishing. Fishing message boards, bait shop updates, and just asking fellow anglers can point you in the right direction. You also don't necessarily need to go far. Many small streams, lakes, and ponds, even those in urban environments, often hold fish. So look close to home first. If you are on a fishing trip in an area you don't know well, head to the closest bait shop and ask for fishing advice.

FINDING THE FISH

Even if you don't have a depth-finder, fish cameras, or other gadgets, you can make a well-informed guess on where the fish are; fish like to hide, so they are often found where there is cover. They often congregate where there are shifts or objects in the environment. Some examples: rocks near open water, weeds near open water, open water surrounded by weeds, swirling current near a straight current, still water near moving water, and so on.

A largemouth bass hiding amid a rocky bottom

POSSIBLE FISH LOCATIONS ON A STREAM OR A RIVER

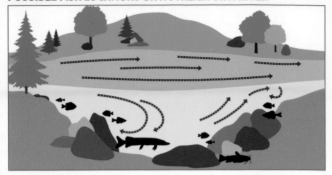

POSSIBLE FISH LOCATIONS IN A LAKE

VARYING DEPTH

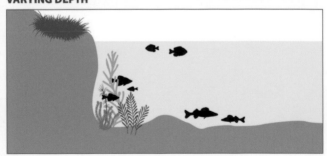

Fish are not always found at the same depth, often moving up and down in the water column in search of prey or more suitable temperatures or oxygen levels. If you lack electronic fish finders, and aren't having luck at one depth, try varying the depth at which you're fishing.

GETTING A BITE

It is not hard to tell you have a fish when a large pike smashes your lure as you drag it across the surface of a still lake. It is not so easy when a big bluegill is absconding with a cricket or a worm from your hook. That's where bobbers come in; a bobber's motion alerts you to what's happening underwater. With practice, you'll be able to set the hook before the bobber is pulled under and the fish swallows the hook or spits the bait out. If you're not using a bobber, you have to watch for (and feel) the "take" by the line's action when a fish starts to move with a bait. Watching how the line (and the rod tip) moves can be a real help here, but learning the feel of a bite will nab you the most fish.

Black Crappie

SETTING THE HOOK

The act of hooking a fish is called "setting the hook," and it is something of an art; even experienced anglers don't always hook fish every time. After a fish takes the bait (lures are considered bait) into its mouth, it does one of two things: swallows it or spits it out. You need to set the hook—and embed the hook in its mouth—before it does either.

How to Set a J Hook and Lures

- Point the rod tip toward the fish.
- Reel in a bit, taking the slack out of the line.
- Sweep the rod over your head quickly, bending the rod.
- Start reeling in the fish.

How to Set Circle Hooks

- Point the rod tip toward the fish.
- Reel in a bit, taking the slack out of the line.
- Smoothly and slowly pull the rod back, letting the bend in the rod do the work.
- Start reeling in the fish.

LANDING A SMALLER FISH

Most of the time smaller fish can just be reeled in and grabbed, but for larger fish, you might need a net and some help.

Sunfish

- Land the fish quickly; this minimizes the stress on the fish.

- Avoid lifting a large fish solely with your fishing rod; as this can break your rod.

- Be sure larger fish are worn down before attempting to land them.

- When netting a fish, keep the fish's head up and scoop it from below.

LANDING A LUNKER

If the fish is large and your tackle is light, the challenge is on and the sport begins. Here are a few tips for bigger fish:

- Keep the line tight.

- Anytime the fish is not taking line off the reel against the drag, you should be reeling in.

- Let the rod bend, taking the shock of the fight.

- If the fish is pulling too much line from the rod, you may have to adjust the drag during the fight.

- With very big fish and heavy tackle, you may have to pump the rod by pulling the tip up, then reeling in line as you lower the rod.

- Gently bring the fish toward you; if you're on a boat or a dock, try not to let it go underneath (as you can lose a fish this way).

- Ideally, you'll have a companion holding a net at water level.

Muskie

There are many popular game and sport fish found throughout the U.S., but the following groups are especially popular or common. Here are some tips to help you identify—and hopefully land—your catch!

BASS FAMILY (*Micropterus* genus)

Description: Elongated oval body with large forward-facing mouth; stiff spines and soft rays in a single dorsal fin; pectoral fins over pelvic fins; slightly forked tail

Well-Known Varieties: Largemouth Bass, Smallmouth Bass, Spotted Bass

Where: Largemouth and Spotted Bass prefer weedy cover in lakes, ponds, and sluggish streams; Smallmouth bass are found near rocks and logs in cool, clear lakes and fast streams.

Equipment: Spinning rod with 8-12 pound monofilament line or a baitcasting rod with braided line if fishing amid heavy cover

Rig: Suspended rigs with live bait

Bait: Live, active baits, such as frogs, leeches, or minnows; large flashy plugs, spinners, plastic worms or frogs

Tip: Suspend crayfish in weedbed openings, or let one drift into stream eddies.

SUNFISH (*Lepomis* genus)

  Description: Deep flat body; small mouth; stiff spines and soft rays in a single dorsal fin; pectoral fins over pelvic fins; slightly forked tail

  Well-Known Varieties: Bluegill, Green, Longear, Pumpkinseed, Redear (Shellcracker)

  Where: Weedy cover

  Equipment: Spinning rod with 4–6 pound monofilament line

  Rig: Suspended rigs with live baits

  Bait: Worms, crickets, leeches; small jigs

  Tip: Combine a single kernel of sweet corn with a cricket for bigger fish.

CRAPPIE (*Pomoxis* Genus)

  Description: Deep, flat body; large mouth; stiff spines and soft rays in a single dorsal fin; pectoral fins over pelvic fins; slightly forked tail

  Well-Known Varieties: Black Crappie, White Crappie

  Where: Black Crappies are found near weedy cover; White Crappies are found in more open water.

  Equipment: Spinning rod with 4–6 pound monofilament line

  Rig: Suspended rigs with live bait or small artificial bait

  Bait: Minnows; small jigs

  Tip: Try tipping a jig with a wax worm.

TROUT (Multiple genera)

    Description: Long, round body; small fleshy top fin near tail

    Well-Known Varieties: Rainbow Trout, Brown Trout, Brook Trout

    Where: Edges of current and deep pools in clear streams; open water in stocked lakes

    Equipment: Spinning rod with 4-6 pound monofilament line; fly rods

    Rig: Bottom rigs

    Bait: Worms; small spinners, flies

    Tip: Fishing a small grasshopper near the surface can work.

WALLEYE AND SAUGER (*Sander* genus)

    Description: Long, round body; mouth with teeth; two dorsal fins; pectoral fins over pelvic fins; slightly forked tail

    Well-Known Varieties: Walleye; Sauger

    Where: Near the bottom, close to rocks or weedy cover

    Equipment: Spinning rod with 6-10 pound monofilament line

    Rig: Bottom rigs with live bait

    Bait: Minnows, leeches; jigs tipped with live bait

    Tip: Fish outside weed bed edges just as darkness falls.

PIKE (*Esox* genus)

> **Description:** Long, round body; large toothy mouth
>
> **Well-Known Varieties:** Northern, Muskellunge, Pickerel
>
> **Where:** Weedy cover near open water
>
> **Equipment:** Spinning rod with 12–20 pound monofilament line; a baitcasting rod with braided line
>
> **Rig:** Suspended rigs
>
> **Bait:** Minnows; large plugs, spinners and spoons
>
> **Tip:** Use a large minnow amid weed bed openings.

CATFISH (Multiple genera)

> **Description:** Big head with chin barbels; no scales
>
> **Well-Known Varieties:** Channel, White, Flathead, Bullhead
>
> **Where:** Bottom near deep water
>
> **Equipment:** Baitcasting rod (with braided line)
>
> **Rig:** Bottom
>
> **Bait:** Cut bait, minnows; prepared bait
>
> **Tip:** Fish large dead minnows at night near weedy cover.

CARP (multiple genera)

Description: Thick body, sucker mouth, forked tail; while not popular table fare with every angler, carp are large, common fish and fun to catch

Well-Known Varieties: Common, Grass

Where: Still water near weedy cover

Equipment: Spinning rod or a baitcasting rod with 10-20 pound monofilament line

Rig: Bottom rigs

Bait: Worms; prepared bait

Tip: Flavor dough balls with strawberry Jell-O, and fish under a very small bobber.

PERCH (*perca* genus)

Description: Elongated body with two dorsal fins; yellow body with 6 to 9 dark vertical bars

Well-Known Varieties: Yellow Perch

Where: Open water in clear lakes and streams

Equipment: Spinning rod with 4-6 pound monofilament line

Rig: Suspended rigs with live bait or small artificial baits

Bait: Minnows, worms, and leeches; small jigs

Tip: Fish a yellow jig with a small worm near the bottom.

CATCH-AND-RELEASE

Letting your fish go (known as catch-and-release) allows you to enjoy the sport without harming the resource. Catch-and-release is especially important for overharvested species and protecting large breeding females. Catch-and-release is only truly successful if the fish survives the experience. To ensure survivability:

- Play and land fish quickly.

- Wet your hands before touching the fish.

- Handle the fish gently and return it to the water quickly.

- Don't hold the fish by the eyes or gills.

- If the fish is deeply hooked, cut the line so 1 inch hangs out of the mouth.

EATING FISH

Eating your catch is one of the joys of fishing. Before you sit down to dinner, be aware that some waters are impaired (either due to mercury contamination or other pollutants). Check with your local natural resource agencies for fish consumption advisories before consuming fish.

For the best-tasting fish, you'll need to keep fish as fresh as possible, so once you've cleaned the fish (see below), get it on ice quickly.

Also, if you're planning on transporting your fish, check your state's regulations about transporting cleaned fish.

PREPARING WHOLE FISH

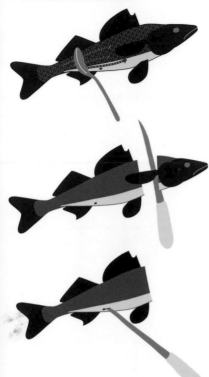

- Scale the fish by holding the tail against a tabletop and running a spoon across the scales toward the head.

- Cut the head off just behind the gills.

- Open the body cavity by slitting the fish from the vent up to the head. Remove the entrails, fins, and the gills if the head is left on.

FILLETING FISH

- Starting from just behind the gills, cut down and just to (but not through) the backbone.

- Slice through the fish horizontally from the head to the tail, along and just above the backbone; stop your cut just before you reach the tail.

- Repeat both steps on the other side of the fish.

- With the skin side of the fillet down, slide the knife between the skin and the flesh, separating the fillet from the skin.

- Cut off any remaining fins.